A Careful Contrition

A Careful Contrition

poems by

Gary Glauber

Shanti Arts Publishing
Brunswick, Maine

A Careful Contrition

Copyright © 2021 Gary Glauber

All rights reserved. No part of this book may be
used or reproduced in any manner whatsoever
without the prior written permission of the publisher
except for brief quotations in critical reviews
and other uses permitted by copyright law.

Published by Shanti Arts Publishing
Designed by Shanti Arts Designs

Cover image by Ian on unsplash.com; rose by
Stiller Beobachter on Wikimedia Commons

Shanti Arts LLC
193 Hillside Road
Brunswick, Maine 04011
shantiarts.com

Printed in the United States of America

ISBN: 978-1-951651-60-2 (softcover)

Library of Congress Control Number: 2021931761

For my students:

in awe of their fresh pursuits of truth and happiness,
in gratitude for teaching me how to stay young
in a world of constant change and challenges.

Contents

Acknowledgments   9

LIMITATIONS . . .
  This Tall   15
  Displaced   16
  Renaissance   17
  Directionless Decade   18
  Placement   20
  On Fleek   22
  Trick of the Lights   23
  Invention   24
  The Song Plays On   25
  Bound By Convention   26
  You Know The Song   27
  Playlist   28

ADORATIONS
  Apogee   33
  Comes Alive   34
  Companionship   36
  Under the Weather   37
  Chronic Solitude   38
  Discretion   40
  Sacrificial Crumbles   42
  Dystopia: The Musical   44
  Evening Broadcast   45
  Monsoon   47
  Climate Change   49
  Discipline   50

IMPLICATIONS
  Propagation   55
  New World   56
  Near the Zoo   58

Nebulae	60
Hard Times Hit the Garden	62
The Pain Artist	64
Sublimation	68
Contrail	69
Take it on faith, take it to the heart	70
Brunch	72
Awaiting the Deal	74
Long Walk Home	77
Archaeology	78
Superman Agonistes	80
Selling the Stunt	82
Male Order	84
Collapse of the Center	85
Geometry	86

Salvations

Contingent Occurrence	91
Exit Strategy	92
The Uncoupling	93
*Met*aphor	94
Siren	96
Soft Magic	99
Deliver Us from What We've Become	101
Caesura	103
Cathedral	106
Volume Two	107
Macchu Pichu of Your Mind	108
Resignation	109
Alchemy	110
Zeros	111
Dunwoodie	112
Reminder #17	114
Indirections	115
Postscript	116

Acknowledgments

Many thanks to the kind editors of the following journals in which these poems first appeared:

Alexandria Quarterly: "Directionless Decade"
And So Yeah: "Sacrificial Crumbles," "Dunwoodie"
Ariel Chart: "Geometry," "The Uncoupling"
BlogNostics: "Deliver Us From What We've Become"
Breadcrumbs Magazine: "Nebulae, as Breadcrumb #494," "Soft Magic, as Breadcrumb #404"
Deep Water Literary Journal: "Invention," "Under the Weather," "Cathedral"
Event Horizon Magazine: "Climate Change," "Resignation"
First Literary Review – East: "Indiscretion"
Foliate Oak Literary Magazine: "This Tall"
Former People Journal: "Near the Zoo"
In Between Hangovers: "Displaced," "Zeros"
Indiana Voice Journal: "Apogee," "Volume Two"
Literary Nest: "Chronic Solitude"
Mad Swirl: "The Song Plays On"
'Merica Magazine: "Metaphor"
Mojave River Press & Review: "Propagation"
Our Poetry Archive: "Playlist"
Outlaw Poetry: "Superman Agonistes"
Rose Red Review: "Macchu Pichu of Your Mind"
Sheila-Na-Gig: "Take it on faith, take it to the heart," "Postscript"
Sick Lit Magazine: "Renaissance," "On Fleek"
Silver Birch Press: "Comes Alive"

Silver Stork Magazine: "Discipline," "Reminder #17"
Synchronized Chaos: "Trick of the Lights," "New World"
The Paragon Journal: "Contingent Occurrence"
The Piker Press: "Evening Broadcast," "Brunch"
The Scarlet Leaf Review: "You Know the Song," "Companionship," "Male Order"
Third Wednesday: "Bound by Convention"
Tin Lunchbox Review: "Dystopia: The Musical," "Exit Strategy"
True Chili: "Awaiting the Deal"
Tuck Magazine: "Contrail"
Verse-Virtual Magazine: "Discretion," "Collapse of the Center," "Caesura"
Vita Brevis Poetry Magazine: "Long Walk Home," "Alchemy"
West Trade Review: "Archaeology"
Writers Resist: "Sublimation"

One
LIMITATIONS

This Tall

Her profile says she wants
a man of a certain height,
and even though he finds her
more than attractive,
he is not tall enough to qualify.
It reminds him of being
in that amusement park
with his older brother and his friends.
He remembers not making the mark
when he had to stand there
alongside the wooden sign that read,
"You must be this tall to ride."
Again, height was a barrier.
There would be no
roller coaster excursions
at this juncture,
no chance to experience
the stomach-churning drops
when hearing her talk
about her last relationship,
no thrilling screams when
their easy romance took
an impossible twist
for no discernible reason.
Instead, he sits in another
giant teacup, pondering the different
world of shorter people,
twisting the middle controller
to steer cup to spin and spin,
making the world a dizzy blur
of inadvertent movement
where height becomes
one of many random things
that no longer matter.

Displaced

Trying to make sense
out of newfangled chaos,
places that no longer exist,
all in the name of progress.
Each day brings us further along,
farther away from what was.
Now gaze upon this blurred haze,
where even shadows look unfamiliar.
Equal and opposite,
polar and bipolar,
magnetic and repulsive,
change the only constant.
Consistently different,
years erase memories
and remnants get picked over
in poor charade of
forging bravely on
toward a mecca
no one dare recognize.

Renaissance

Thirty seconds turns to thirty years:
crying in the rain,
looking for a cab uptown.
Moods of books read infect you;
storefronts and colored signs
provide clues for body and mind
through thoughts abraded by absence
and that pair of white travel pants.
Ambition has gone the way of consequence.
The poetic possibility of these many years
goes unrealized, thwarted by assumptions,
frustrated by excitement and the inexact
mercurial nature of words.
Beauty and doubt coexist
and when I tell you, "Never change,"
it is clear you already have.
There is no cause for grief here.
You assure me this is the natural progression.
Simple turns complex and agitated.
Even a walk in the park
seems cursed with careful orchestration.
You catalog my weaknesses
as if to defy how time brings change,
yet the real gift goes unspoken,
captured in our tired embrace,
hugging for a moment longer,
a firm defense against
inevitable passage of years.

Directionless Decade

It was a precarious hell,
an age of fearmongerers,
terrible and simple.
Safety was not a prime concern,
and we all watched for signals,
ignoring the few caveats
and going with the flow.
Education was a useless concept,
and theorems proved nothing.
It was common and familiar,
a time of heightened desire.
Everyone talked about big ideas
and love and peace as solutions.
They roused rabble and raised tarnation,
traded spouses
and amplified music
to vibrant point of pain.
They sang of revolution
and emotions and change.
Yet in the end,
very little occurred.
Problems did not get solved
and ideals were sold
as hard capital.
In the end,
it was never quite as good
as people remembered it being,
and everyone was there.
We traveled to distant worlds
and back again,

and all we recall now is
a need for seat belts
and labeled warnings,
hearkened nods to nostalgia
while heeding the future's
clarion collect call.

Placement

It's a world comprised of things:
some endearing, others less so.
Windows protect us from
the outside, its dangerous knowledge,
its singular evils and freedoms,
life's lucid dream gone awry.

You sit there, cruel and judgmental,
an émigré quick to decide what's better
for everyone in the longest run:
truth so unrealistic.

Tell us again about that time
you fled suffocating country
to find new ways to forget,
a moving target
at home between pages of news ink
and photos of cozy tourist destinations.
Life becomes a steamy postcard
you were never brave enough to send.

You ride the wild coaster into oblivion,
spinning into dizzy circles of answers you seek
(or at least shadows in which they're hidden).

Keep those strong hands at bay,
who can say what they might touch?
Even perfection. One never knows
where the sand will fall, what strange designs
form in this reckless wind
of beautiful emergence.

It's the middle ages of this cloistered existence.
You step away from the door to hide
but loneliness still tracks you
like a homing pigeon chasing crumbs
of yesterday's misinformation.
Left out to dry, on sale for a discount,
bartered to the trade for some unholy swap
of uncomfortable silences.

We clear the cache and begin again,
paying more attention to punctuation,
clues that might tell us how to feel
this time, the only time, when tide rolls in
unassuming and destructive,
covering our tracks,
burying needles beneath
sounds of crashing waves,
the auditory lull that,
in its perfect repetition,
is easily mistaken for peace.
People shout and your silence
answers harshly.

You close the window
and cry yourself to sleep
in the same rhythms
of that beloved poem
you once heard a mother sing
to her sick child
on the crowded uptown train.
Eyes swollen; you look around
at the things surrounding,
and they still make up a world.

On Fleek

We roam far out of our way,
preserving illusions of independence.
We debate what's normal
but fear becoming that cliché.
We pick up cues, lay down buzzwords
like seeds in springtime.
Dark and bizarre, odd souls
smart enough to make scammers hesitate
before unveiling the tired charade
of being robbed so far from home,
tragic, beyond tragic,
hubris and a portfolio of flaws,
we sigh politely, and silently post
another ironic Instagram,
making do with what we have.
Here is freedom.
This is our empty veranda,
these the retro porch chairs,
here we meander off the trail,
holding collective breaths,
awaiting distant shimmer
of that gilded glowing epiphany,
realization as event,
visual proof of feelings felt,
lives lived in six-second increments,
our postmodern legacy.

Trick of the Lights

Watching you slowly sip espresso
is one of life's great pleasures
in the curtained dark mahogany
of this bohemian village café,
playing out artistic cliché.
The comfortable silence
of your company
after these many years
of shared lives, jobs,
relationship problems and triumphs,
disillusion, confusion, misplaced
sarcasm as self-protection
against wry new century
is soporific balm, panacea.
You recommend a good podcast;
I write clues on napkins.
Together, we try to figure things out.
Small things are key to survival:
a dark French roast is aromatic win,
another shared victory
of time and persistence
where one plus one is much more
than a pair fighting the uncaring
bright lights of biggest city,
its urban sprawl of fear and loneliness
taking prisoners every moment,
spitting out the defeated
who caved to the struggle
without sharing the misery
in a way that doesn't merely
love company, but also
provides strength.

Invention

Orpheus had the right idea,
start with what you know,
who you are, the intricacy
of your particular predicament.

As those waiting for inspiration
grow old and soddenly shapeless,
you dream of agile French girls
dancing agitation into bonhomie.

Writing is three parts elucidation
of self-confidence trapped in nature.
Walk slowly, pay careful attention;
see where that brick wall holds the love.

Feed the senses in a primitive way,
holding component words at bay,
arranging, displaying, inveighing
in search of form marrying content.

Like the swirling torrent of gusty wind,
it is soon beyond you, a missed moment,
a sleeper's contrition in light of wasted day,
despondent dilemma turned endless apology.

The Song Plays On

Stuck in a unidirectional flow,
staring at ocean view out our window,
sharing wisps of last night's dreams,
connecting to colors, old melodies,
a wide realm of touchstones,
spinning lack into another great maybe.
Abundance is here, merely hiding,
waiting around nearest corner,
whistling a happy refrain.
That cloud looks like a heron,
a sign of hope, omen of portent,
potent with potential, a coda
full of unresolved possibility:
wanting warmth, needing love,
not ready for requiem yet.

Bound by Convention

After being held hostage so long,
I was happy to be back, smiling.
At the pawn shop, I stopped and
asked Hank whether he still had
anything left from the haul I conscripted.
He showed me the Tunisian dartboard,
the emerald cufflinks, and that
striped cummerbund that once
proclaimed eminent domain.
I'm getting out of politics, I told him,
and he nodded, not believing me.
People seemed hesitant to talk to me,
perhaps because they had heard so many
speak my name on radio and TV.
At Sally's, looking for the same old crowd,
I was sadly disappointed. I was hungry
for familiar banter, the kind of easy rapport
I was known for: precise, biting, breezy.
In months of dark damp rooms I practiced
nonchalance as a means of survival.
Now free in a world indifferent
to panache and presence,
this was a pretty place devoid of emotion.
The investigation was ongoing,
my life constantly dusted for prints,
everyone seeking rhymes forgoing reason.
The old man on the bench looked lost,
and seemed to like that estranged feeling.
He held the mirror up to my questions.
I breathed hard at first, then realized
I was back, a fixture, a landmark, a
totem of discrete and relative reality,
more than halfway home.

You Know the Song

Invention turned intervention.
Nights of silent screams and slow motion shadows.
This is not a game, she says.

Into the treacherous badlands,
playing with money, playing for keeps
until the time someone sets up rules.

Driven by the impressive bass line,
you rise to the call and response
like a perfect three-part harmony.

Even the Sphinx had an inkling
of the larger meaning behind it all.
You stretch and feign disinterest.

Science is an art here, math a simple fraction
of all your promised potential. You break
as though life had a solo to offer.

In the repeating chorus,
she begs you to think.
Think about heartache.

You are called from your hiding place
into the heat of a radiating spotlight,
the world of the greater world.

The coda repeats and fades.
The backup singers express remorse.
You try to find a verse to save you.

Playlist

My music library is chock full
of melodic souvenirs left
by those whose lives
ended unfairly early.
I'm not talking your typical
rock star overdose,
nor run-of-the mill consequence
of hard partying years
taking consequential toll.
While I've my fair share of those,
my list is more erudite:
the soulful young artist
who died from a rare strain
of testicular cancer mere months
after piecing together a debut album,
the gifted British chanteuse
cut down in her prime while vacationing
by a speedboat's propellers –
wrong place, wrong time;
the prog-rock genius who died
from auto-erotic asphyxiation
just as his career was taking off,
the Tennessee guitarist whose
upbeat and optimistic songs
belie facts of his life's battles
with relentless depression,
ending in the silence of suicide.
The list goes on, nuanced,
brilliant, and underappreciated,
a heavenly roster of talents
who could fill a festival's slots
for days on end,

a ghostly Woodstock
of those who shed this mortal coil
prematurely, but left tunes
I still listen to endlessly
in gracious appreciation
of how the art of music
outlasts tenuous promise
of earthly survival.

Two
ADORATIONS

Apogee

Let this small world of ours keep spinning
against growing crowd of disbelievers,
despite mounting odds, circumstantial invention,
and desperate forces that feed on ego drama.
They tell us dreams don't count, they fade and fracture,
but we know secrets to prove the contrary.
This delicate orbit holds in a sweet and fragile balance,
a gyroscopic vision of richly colored silks and textured velvets
that vibrates as thrum of underwater signal,
a pleasant convergence of heart and mind,
body and soul, music and language, truth and belief.
It is a house of cards that withstands inner riot,
angst of a million small disappointments, and
barriers imagined by those governing powers past.
We find faith in each other, in a shared trust,
an inner beauty that transcends cloudy skies
eager to drench others who fear the rain and
stand idly by as drops begin to fall.
Our journey continues on unabated,
protected by the strength of our love,
as we circle the sun together.

Comes Alive

At seventeen, we were a handsome couple,
filled with hope and youthful exuberance,
dreams not yet compromised or diluted,
driving around together, kissing in
shadows of commuter train tracks,
fueling strong urges of innocent lust
at a time before life got complicated.
Your father's death in the rear-view mirror,
your family gathered together in support.
Temporarily I became one of them,
helping you find your way
through adolescence made tougher.
The odometer reflected
the beauty of that dimpled smile
and brown eyes that broadcast
depths of an ocean deep inside.
We touched each other
in any number of ways,
a first love blossoming
to a radio soundtrack
approved by your older brother,
the popularity of Peter Frampton
a sudden revelation after years of touring.
These guitar leads seemed
to show us the way.
I picked you up from a hard shift
at the grocery store,
favorite cashier of the old ladies
and my favorite too.
We drove on, no special destination,
savoring small talk,
the special connection,

miles tallied on the way to
building a relationship.
At seventeen we lived in the moment,
never realizing that someday
we'd run out of gas,
sell the car for scrap metal,
move on to other lives apart.
Back then, the road
stretched on forever.

Companionship

Everything is broken.
Shards of expectation
prove dangerous when
culture surgically removes
familiar notions of native hope.
Barnacles of treacle-laced sentiment
enflame her pretend emotions
to a fevered state, filming the email
to create a stop-motion reminder
of the one time he used that phrase,
evidence of his collateral care,
a magnanimous dispersal of niceties
sent in nonchalant prose.
She wears her hair up,
exudes exotic effortless elegance
and knows what passes for love
in these faraway hallways
collapses under drawn curtains
of passing scrutiny.
She dreams of ancestors
dancing under summer waterfalls,
times when sincere smiles
were the only currency
that ever mattered.
Her mind plays over
desperate exit strategies,
searching for those
that offer respect, freedom from
clown-show anticipation,
this genetic predilection
toward coupling and
this horn of plenty troubles.

Under the Weather

She wore war paint of gesture and nuance
carefully sculpted in the class
where imagined soul meets imaginary road,
a vision quest, a tribal desire,
searching for ways out
of this existential darkness,

A quagmire carried like heavy cloud
over crowded horizons,
groups of frail and pale,
huddled together,
going nowhere in impatient hurry,
selfie sticks at the ready,
sardonic wit as best defense,
rough edges sanded down
with each hour's new posting,
personal information as public declamation
crying wolf into digital wind.

This is the world outside the window,
the miasma she bequeaths you,
brickbats and bloviating sycophants
preaching to numbed and wounded
on park benches opposite dead stumps,
battling heat waves and sad squalor,
shared indifference as nonchalance,
double shots of espresso awakening desire
in veins through skinny over-inked arms
to keep that distant thought of love alive.

Chronic Solitude

A year of imperfect seclusion,
measuring blue of shadows
in hope of understanding.

Nature's profligate ways
trouble and confound, yet
unwieldy chase continues.

This is the year, the evolution,
change of seasons and mind,
the constant search for answers.

Books rife with expert wisdom,
cut with anecdotal memories
of misfortune and imbecility.

Shadows laugh at serious horrors,
destructive valleys within valleys,
Eden's gale winds as afterthought.

These many astute observations
help quit addictions afflicting you,
as you aspire to become transparent.

Questioning the force, the creator,
demanding bloody sacrifice on altar,
this holy curiosity turns real when written.

You search on for the tree on fire,
grazing through intricacy of detail,
bitter at the perversity of abundance.

So you present the solitary illusion,
Gordian knots unraveled through
careful lies of suburban omission.

What matters is the emotional truth,
the water bug that eats the world,
the cat and catechism both,
like Eskimo wisdom forever retold.

Discretion

Eclectic neighbor, rarely home,
a community question mark
and subject of much speculation
shows up barefoot on my doorstep
at eleven, a torn evening gown
of deep indigo, an expression
of confused relief, and a whiff
of gin and whispers, asking for
a few moments of protection.

Foolishly, I cave to curiosity
and drawn to the occasion's oddity,
open up and let her in.

No exotic tale of seduction ensues,
rather snippets of odd rejoinders
quilted together as makeshift conversation,
polite, apologetic, and full of hushed grace.

We would be strangers ever after,
even if she spent this unlucky night,
her bronze wedding anniversary,
sleeping off overdone temporary reveries
alone on our family room's comfy couch,
covered up with Aunt Susan's gift afghan,
quiet sobs soon fading to snores.

It was the neighborly thing to do.

She moved away a month later,
no less a mystery, still considered
a monster of social faux pas,
victim of hushed judgments from afar,
condemned to rumors and hearsay history.

Here in the suburbs we value silence,
saving the world from sordid secrets
in heroic non-heroic daily dealings.
I cannot share much more about it,
but even if I could, I wouldn't.

Sacrificial Crumbles

Giant fiasco leads to loss,
as I knew it might.
His hate is not a quiet dislike.
He runs an active campaign.

So I drink wine,
surround myself with positives,
focus on what good will come.

While not my best self with him,
it was pretty damn good regardless.
Feel compassion for my decisions.

The steeled mindset poisons things
beyond isolation and loneliness.
Unless you've lived this, don't judge.

Your mind is a world beset with worry,
a fiction of too quiet contemplations:
what his day is like, possible futures together.

You buy into the dysfunction,
sign up for unrealistic promises,
ignore actions speaking louder than words.

Today I catalogued my mother's recipe,
one used when baking for my soldier dad,
the same used when baking for him.

She called them "sweet longings."
The sugar, butter, flour, and chocolate
expressed her distant yearnings.

But I cross that out and rename them,
wiser now one generation later,
that cookies don't always sate this urge,
that giving must be its own reward.

Dystopia: The Musical

In this heightened reality, words have no place.
Minor chords convey present troubles and
lyrical swells rise in measured dissonance,
cues for narrating chaos, historic accidents
where dreams collide against harsh reality
and characters fall along wisdom's wayside.

Romance then helped stave off rife insanity
of political turbulence, war's brutal way of
dehumanizing life into actions and orders.
People sought solace in counterfeit encounters,
brief meaningless pleasures that blanketed pain
in illusory promises paid out in hours.

We watch as they are broken, as time limps ahead,
relentless, incensed, world awash in its tears.
Still there are dreams, and searching continues.
In life there are quandaries, no trouble-free solutions,
scenes follow quickly, unthinkable things occur.
No one expects a happy ending.

To what end does this practiced futility lead?
Lessons like lesions placed front and center
to heal our wounded souls, to expose our follies
set to showtunes meant to flourish in memory.
We sing and dance and turn to tomorrow's children,
whose innocent charms soften sharp edges.

Tonight's witnesses are in standing ovation,
appreciative from the safety of distance,
protected and praying that such atrocities
never affect their perfect suburban haven.
This bubble of false hope surrounds us,
yet terror is off-stage smirking, lurking in the wings.

Evening Broadcast

This current
internecine strife,
result of bloated egos
floating downstream
willy-nilly, full of
important hidden agendas.
Back after the tease.

Remember:
loudest sinner
gets first dibs on absolution
from a reading-challenged
puppet-master, forever
unspooling strings from
precocious tangle.

Chaos is style,
dim lamp to light
a path to progress,
the hit and myth
of knuckleball's journey
from press release
to catcher's mitt.

Concessions
at the stand,
compromises
at the ready,
and still purchase
eludes a nation,
stalled in fog
of clever rhetoric.

—continued

While straw men
burn in forests
against green screens
changing, going viral,
it's thrown back
to smiling anchor
reminding
we are complicit
in this together
and wishing all
another good night.

Monsoon

The city was still licking its wounds.
The abandoned corporate headquarters
held shadows the size of airplane hangars.
I was dancing outside those shadows,
carrying clothes to a laundromat,
learning life lessons in how to keep
pink away from what once were white undies.
Life was a roll of quarters then:
long distance calls, detergent, dryers,
the jukebox at local pub.
Quarters and embarrassment.
I lacked basic social cues;
such were the lingering scars
of expired adolescence.
Minimum wage careers loomed
like bad movies shown over and over again
during impossibly late hours
on a black and white TV.
As I tried to shower off
the deep fryer's stale oil stink,
I pondered how the man
became the cartoon fish.
No plot seemed less likely.
Life was a tedious task
repeated to mastery,
and an employee-of-the-week citation.
With taxes taken out,
it seemed even more pointless,
a joke from the universe.
Yet no one laughs.

—continued

Instead force of anger
translates into attitude
and gathering storm front
swirls in whispered frustration.
This is the legacy of loss,
a city seeking oxygen in tired lungs
against somnolence of habit.
Every downpour begins with
one lonely drop crashing down,
eager for company in a world
that only respects thunder.
Even in memory,
everything gets wet.

Climate Change

Hope proceeds in increments,
festooned with numbed sensibility,
and an ever-unreliable narrator.

He trades in stolen memories
and shorts the market each time,
hedging bets against better judgment.

No one expects happy endings,
that went the way of the mullet,
another fashion mistake of the past.

There's a rich supply of cold calculation,
and the numbers are telling lies
all about ego's best kept secrets:

Animal magnetism,
the mother country,
frosting on the beater.

So she looks for a replacement
amidst what comes along
at parties full of assurances.

Past all this too shall pass
she never quite believes it,
having wasted years in anticipation.

Where is that something else?
The window frames disappointment
and an unhealthy amount of rain.

Discipline

for James Tate

Want to make you laugh,
then break your heart automatically.
Such activities can be rewarding.

You won't fit me into a square little box.
My narrative is ever expanding.
We are beyond understanding.

We all want to step out of this tired life,
but evidence disputes such miracles.
Ultimately, it's what life is all about.

Universal frailty and indecision:
perplexed, befuddled, trapped,
and somehow stuck in-between.

Fear and anxiety over something
unknown, you didn't see coming.
Let's pretend it's all imaginary.

The problem is that we don't belong
to any place, any tradition.
Life is a small town, wherever you are.

You experience hideous upheaval,
reversals of expectations,
wonder what happens next.

This world spins out of control:
we become people undreamed,
speaking an evolved hard slang.

You can't do anything about it.
We push it to the extreme,
seeking to learn along the way.

Silence crouches in,
tension keeps things moving,
We concentrate on overhearing others.

It's poignant to realize
how crazy this world is,
how you must never give in.

The challenge is to avoid the tears,
have fun with the daily horror.
Let's have a good day if we can.

Three

IMPLICATIONS

Propagation

Disappointment slows her down,
knocks her off that perch of high desire.

So she turns to nature first,
seeking solace in reciting

a liturgy of fancy flower names
like hot Latin whispers in the night.

Sweet bougainvillea glabra,
azaleas to span a noisy rainbow.

Next she prays on her rosary,
lights the votive for selfish gain,

contrary to its higher purpose.
Another sin added to her tally.

This is ignorance, I tell her.
With *benefits*, she corrects me.

There is nothing simpler
than an array of arrogant beliefs.

She seeks lengthy apologies,
divine intervention as retribution.

The sun circles an oblate disc
as wiser heads shake, prevailing,

admiring colorful clusters,
traversing the quiet long corridor.

New World

My student reveals
some online stranger
has offered her forty dollars
for a picture of her tongue.
The screens are up,
and sorry Pandora,
but there's no logging out,
no signing off from this
global highway where
connections facilitate
judgments by the nanosecond.
Devices thwart agency,
glowing like sideshow mirrors,
presenting images of avatars
in forums where being liked
is the post-modern mecca.
You are whoever in
whatever way possible,
but even more so, yet
there's no escaping you.
Genuinely modified personas
haunt this alien nation,
a unique brand of connected
isolation, where attention spans
are shrinking alongside
antiquated notions of
what once was privacy.
It's a visual visceral
celebration of simulated shallow,
first worlders pondering problems
from skewed perspective, programmed
for individual enjoyment,

looking down at lowly collective
as mere historical footnote,
now that fame is cheap
and often inexplicable,
a host of followers
eagerly toasting
the odd as pseudo art,
never bothering to read
updated terms of agreement.

Near the Zoo

She tells me about crazy times
after hours when she was a dental assistant,
making love in those reclining dental chairs,
the challenge of finding ever new positions.
She was young then, prone to drinking a bit.
Besides, she says, her first husband
was always traveling, giving boardroom
pep talks in lands she'll never visit.
He did give her a son, however, and
every three or four years he remembers
to call on his birthday. He still doesn't
know his son is gay. But how am *I* doing?
Her new husband is far nicer, a semi-retired
financial whiz whose hobby is gardening.
She speaks of his lactose intolerance,
how it has forced her away from the
rich dairy desserts she had been known for
back in her culinary phase.
We traverse the garden paths of this
nature conservancy, and she talks about
her days abroad, the restlessness
a bucolic village incites, the way it
makes her appreciate the hectic chaos
of London she once despised.
Did I know she once survived a year
only on modeling fees from classes
at a small nearby art university?
She says a large audience prevents
her from feeling totally naked.
But *were you?* She smiles,
and that is answer enough.
These remind me of Monet, she says.

Those aren't water lilies.
Close enough, she says.
Is it too early for wine?
I am suddenly thinking about
exotic animals, how they can
be put on leashes, but never tamed.
She has to get back to the hotel soon,
because her husband will wonder
what has become of her.
That is an excellent question.

Nebulae

There's a vague sublimity to the whole endeavor.
We could be anywhere or anyone:
vacationers on rented time, casting reckless shadows.

Our boredom defines us like generational motto.
The last original movie was made thirty years before.
Everything animated has been updated to live action.

We are waiting for someone to bring our lives to action,
to remind us friends are not merely extras,
actors for hourly hire eager for security of work.

Together we explore sideline concepts of beauty
as related to a sad nearby water park.
We fear our own laughter while waiting in line.

This is a dark cloud of discovery:
your hillbilly past, my parental abandonment,
yet we toast our childhood challenges together

and float down what they call "the lazy canal,"
a twisted backwoods Fellopian nightmare
with trance music piped in.

This is as close to nature as we'll ever get,
our own natures as well,
though we both like watching the weather.

It's a seasonal pilgrimage
undertaken like some Ambien incident,
forgotten instantly, except for the heat.

We're the new artificial wilderness,
substance formed via connected stories
that vanish like meaning after a day.

In the end, there is nothing left
but two contiguous bodies
watching cloud formations

as they turn into messages
that foretell of a prescient world
where everything suddenly matters.

Hard Times Hit the Garden

Slowly, the neighborhood changes
in imperceptible ways:
fewer trees, more cement,
a heaviness that lingers,
fluorescents every few feet
on concrete thoroughfares,
chain link fences clattering
in midnight windstorms.

This is your broken bottle.
your empty threat,
explosion waiting to happen.

The cage bars are there for your protection;
hours of rage filled with sharp inflection,
voices off-stage leading insurrection.

What could never happen
happens.

It's no accident.

The saber's rattle,
ancient battle
renewed.

A progression
of decadence abandoned
to rot and careless ruin,
subversive underclass
whose rage assaults
former magnificence

as though answering
personal attacks.

Abase, deface, set chase, erase.

Pray for grace.

Time the great equalizer.
Time the true liberator,
master and slave both yoked
to linear circle as history repeats.

And seasons
in their cycle
pass baton,
come undone
yet stumble on,
unlikely as spring

rain
endless rain
flooding rain
stagnant rain
always rain

as we all
soak in sad knowledge,
then strive to become.

The Pain Artist

I
Blue house small-town birth
to an abundance of names,
this daughter of a painter's son
was always close to her father.
Her Catholic mother was his second wife,
and gave him four more daughters.
He already had two.
Frida was next to last,
born into a world of females.

Her birth was like a revolution.
Gunfire echoed in the streets.
Revolutionaries leapt over walls
into her backyard, where her mother.
would be waiting with a hot meal.

At six, a bout with polio left
her right leg thinner than the left.
Soon came a lifetime of long skirts.

II
At an elite school for girls,
she became an agile boxer.
Violent struggles surrounded her.
The revolution continued,
so she joined a gang,
fell in love with the leader.

III
An accident
changed everything.

Bus collided with trolley:
broken spinal column,
collarbone, ribs, pelvis;
eleven right leg fractures;
dislocated foot and shoulder;
iron handrail pierced her
abdomen and uterus.
Pain forevermore.
Extreme pain.

IV
For three months,
a full body cast
left her immobilized.
She turned away from
studying medicine
toward painting,
a means to occupy
a wounded body's
active heart and mind.

Self-portraits
punctuated time
between 35 surgeries.
It was the subject
she knew best.
Alone with a special easel
and mirror, she painted in bed.

Stark portrayals of pain
translated, transformed

—continued

with bright colors
and dramatic symbolism.
A strange reality of wounds
physical and psychological:
marriage, miscarriages,
pain, operations,
lustful monkeys
and Mexican culture
through surrealist filter.
The Louvre purchased
one painting.

V
Unibrow beauty
seeks artistic advice,
winds up a wife.
He has a flourishing career.
He recognizes her talent.
Intimacy, then marriage:
Elephant weds Dove.

Fire meeting fire
turns tumultuous.
He had affairs;
she had affairs.
Bisexual affairs,
heterosexual affairs.
He slept with her sister.
They divorced.
They remarried.
Nothing changed.
Maelstrom after maelstrom.

VI

Trotsky fled from Stalin
right into Frida's arms.
His wife wasn't happy.
They moved elsewhere.
Trotsky was assassinated.
A love of politics
can get far too real.

VII

Gangrene took her right leg,
amputated at the knee.
She kept fighting against
the growing tab of injury's debt.
Broncho-pneumonia left
her frailer yet. Soon death
came calling. She was 47.
Today the blue house
holds the urn with her ashes.

But the real legacy
is the merited heritage
of paintings left behind,
emerging from shadows,
finally getting their due,
showing us the pain,
the unique reality
of the wondrously talented
Frida.

Sublimation

He enthusiastically supports
the man whose conflated policies
can thwart and negate him
because he is living proof
Willy Loman did not die in vain.
He sells; he is well-liked.
It's Muslim with a small m,
no Nation of I action here.
His string of successes
is tied tightly to the capitalist
benefits of fossil fuels
and a planet slowly dying.
His carbon footprint
leaves divots the world over
and yet, invited to become a member
of prestigious country club,
he jumps at the chance.
Eighteen holes to prove
he is an example, an exception,
paraded around as proof,
a minority friend and
he willingly looks the other way,
focusing instead on movie star
shaking hands gladly
across the banquet hall.
Every photo op
is his small revenge,
and he who laughs last
lives to laugh another day,
even when things get serious fast.
Life is funny like that
and compromise is the new normal,
alternate facts showing how
bleak is the new black.

Contrail

Vienna waits for no man,
meanwhile one in seat E11
cannot stop his own jet propulsion.

In a flurry of ongoing strokes,
he paints an olfactory nightmare,
a Pollack of odors within enclosed space.

When some ask him to stop,
he cannot. The gaseous state
is a fugue, a fog, an invitation to action.

They complain louder, longer.
The flight crew alerts the pilot
and a warning is issued, only

it is to those gasping for clean air,
not the one polluting the cabin.
Everyone has a right to flatulence.

An emergency landing occurs.
Four complainants are removed:
a case of "fart for fart's sake."

The crew assures those remaining
that this was for their own safety,
that altercations are what really stink
as they take off to high heaven.

Take it on faith, take it to the heart

We all wait for death, one student says,
as if you rise in unison, all Hemingway-esque
to daily declare, "Today is a good day to die."
But you don't. You are suburban children
of privilege. More likely you'll wait the
agonizing two weeks for results
of your SAT or ACT to arrive.
Come fall, you will wait eagerly,
anxiously to hear from
the college of your choice.
As Tom Petty once reminded us,
"The waiting is the hardest part."
You wait for your birthday every year,
waiting to see what special gifts
have come your way.
You'll wait to see if your parents allow you
to go away un-chaperoned for Spring Break.
You'll wait to see who will invite you to prom;
you'll wait to see that no one is wearing
what you have so fashionably chosen.
You'll wait for the light to change
(or maybe you won't, as some suggest).
You'll wait for some change, for completion,
for satisfaction, for amusement
to deliver you from dreaded boredom.
You wait for the bell to ring so that
you'll be granted release from this
relentless grilling on the ways you
wait and the inherent weight of
the anticipation, the pause that
does not refresh, the ecstatic agony
invested with hope, the slow march

of time that propels us in one direction,
leading inevitably to prove that student's
glib reply to be 100, from to be to
not to be. We can wait, you'll tell me.

Brunch

Here's the thing, she said,
apropos of nothing:
Life is a series of moments.

I have had a few
strung together, enough
to give a sense of animation.

She tells me about
the day her daughter knew
she wanted to be an actress.

Every word illuminated
with a parent's pride,
tinged with hope and fear.

I could foresee moments
of cattle calls, of sacrifice,
of art seeking commerce.

Yet there was nothing to say,
sipping the dark roast
rapidly losing its power.

The windows showed
Sunday morning tableaus
that she once adored.

Calm before storm
was the forecast
and as a cloud burst,

that thunder's crack
released a flood of feelings
and strong connections.

It washed up gutters,
deepened all colors
made whispers shout.

We are the water's
flow this ravenous day,
rushing along with memories.

She wipes tears away,
leaves a generous tip,
and taxis rescue us,

going different ways.

Awaiting the Deal

A woman plays soft jazz at the piano,
and I am here to meet night rising,
afloat on expectation and prosecco,
closing eyes in hope that the
evening ahead leads toward
a tomorrow unlike any of
thousands I have known.

Already wondering if I can forgive
the haze of disappointment
that inevitably follows, like seeing
that news anchor without her makeup
reaching for a quart of milk
in the wee hours of morning,
a strange disheveled ghost.
I managed then the stone faced
denial of recognition, pretending
to be polite stranger saint of
24/7 grocery store aisle, he who
sees nothing outside of dreams.

The notes trip pleasantly around
lyrics of a journey in smoky blue,
and still I dread the compromise,
the rib given up for companion,
the taste of forbidden fruit,
the serpent's clever insinuation.
Sensuality hovers like a promise
as it must, international intrigue
dominating thoughts of conversation,
the silky allure of some foreign
culture's colorful entreaty.

Reminds me of that sultry
penthouse party at the
pop art icon's commercial behest,
all the pretty people staring out
in mutual admiration, making
important calls that never
quite connected. I read the pain
in the model's eyes before realizing
the actual scars that sang out
to millions on tabloid pages.
I understood how such beauty
might drive a madman
over the edge forever.
It's a world of harsh injustice.
I thanked her for the smile,
but she soon left with another.

At such times, even the familiar
gets lost in a fog of impropriety,
and waking with views of the park
seems Technicolor false, another
postcard from someone's stolen mail,
reality drifting away like those
tiny people out on the street below.
Minor chords invite trepidation,
and I heed their unresolved warnings.

Praying to Gods of blurred boundary,
I ride out elongated hours until dawn,

—continued

playing my part, dressed to the nines
with careful designer flair, on my
impresario's vigil solo, no seconds
in my corner to cajole and encourage
as I mentally recite calculated pitch
and make it sound spontaneous as hell.

This is the curse of my blessing,
the ceaseless stories that form
into a life reflected in shoes well shined.
There's something sentimental here,
worth your long-term investment,
a nine-part documentary of serious intent.
It will offer heartbreak, tenderness,
and currents of social responsibility
discussed from the safe distance of
your offshore havens, the ones
you'll swear never ever exist.
Is that woman still playing?
While I was sitting pondering
a special request for luck,
she appears to have vanished.

Long Walk Home

He climbs to a new depth,
pondering loss with a million
small deliberations and gestures,
so convinced that this hollow keening
heard in distant wind addresses him.
Mrs. Savon still scowls as he passes,
peering from behind jalousied window.
She waggles untoward aged finger,
and curses the same fates
for entirely different reasons.
This is the labor of neighborly judgment,
like when Brownstone's uncle
played Santa at the holiday gathering
with pungent whisky breath
before eventually wetting himself
in a dark and lonely corner.
The whispers of condemnation
were all clearly audible then.
Now the hot pink of Heisel's azalea
suggests he should reconsider:
perhaps fickleness is an
act of nature, the vibrancy of the new
tempting us from staid horizons
into shuddering wilderness
of heightened expectation.
Beauty is temporary, fleeting,
a salvo that propagates passion
with its initial cannon flare,
yet rocks our imprudent courage
as it whizzes by into distracted memory.
Fumbling for keys,
he opens screen door
seeking refuge from himself.

Archaeology

I
I put myself in danger when treading the depths
of your friendship. You are quite deep; I am unskilled.
This is the end for which I was destined:
a beautiful drowning, gasping air
in gossamer dreams, your silken ways
drawing me closer, surrounded by
irresistibly sensual ambrosia.
My kingdom for a boat,
a means by which to circumnavigate
these rocky shoals and emotions.
Your eyes hold secrets your lips never tell.
I wrestle tides, the pull and sway
of heartstrings secured by nautical knots.
I flounder in waves of this bedroom,
the undertow of lusty midnight,
unthinking currents of heady affection.
Swallowing gulps of hard disbelief,
I pray to see next morning.

II
You say you love this, you say you love that.
Your vernacular plays fast and loose with the term
and it loses all meaning.
Morning rain, afternoon sun,
the shape of the moon, the way your head tilts
in that ever-inquisitive pose.
Love love love love.
Each time the word appears,
its symbolism further fades.

III
This garden was here when your grandparents
traded cultural references now lost to the ages.
You recall slicing strawberries with a paring knife,
helping someone with a summer recipe.
Your sweetness, your innocence, renews the world.
Even more so than the shock of that nail polish color
and electric kisses stolen behind the red shed.
This is a fresh dawn of time,
a molten reawakening,
where new land is forming
to bridge the gaps between us,
a torrid continent that may never cool.
From here on, it's about survival.

Superman Agonistes

She stands above me,
shouting out ways
of my insignificance,
telling me how I will die.
Her anger is evident.

I was a hero once.
People loved me
even as I loved myself.
Everything seemed possible.
Back then, it was.

Some promises were broken.
Revenge led to travel,
thinking miles smooth out
hasty acts of angry sorcery,
but you can't escape the past.

New place meant opportunity:
destroyed legacy rebuilt.
I acted swiftly, logically,
currying royal favor
against heavy headwinds.

She was the wild card,
raging fire on dry plain,
enlisting favor from strangers
who'll never know the full tale.
But then, who ever does?

Her unceasing affection
became its own kind of burden,
one I bore quietly, patiently.
Until I didn't,
and hell was delivered.

This dark place
is a seabed of complaint,
chaos, devastation, regret.
Life holds no safe harbor
when pride's poison is revealed.

She rails on,
smug and fast en route
to her next misadventure.
I stay, stigmatized, broken,
redefined as mortal again.

Selling the Stunt

The pose never fails her,
an indifferent come-hither look,
insouciance with hint of smile,
guaranteed to resonate,
inspire lingering longings.
Practiced in the mirror,
it's a tried-and-true fail-safe,
assertion as prevention
from that one time
the so-called boyfriend
decided to dump her.
That sad humiliation
will never be repeated.
She has honed her wiles:
beauty as art, beauty as weapon.
She knows when it's working,
and even when she'd rather it wouldn't.
Like that creepy guy running
for re-election in the county seat
who keeps coming around
when her parents are not home.
She's already told him a better time,
but for him, that better time is now,
hoping to enact some perverse
personal cheerleader fantasy,
where she is super impressed
by his political acumen.
She threatens to call the cops,
slams door in his face.
Life is a series of accumulated incidents,
finding healthy balance between
countering the voluptuous

and working nature's bounty
to greater advantage.
It's not the world's concern,
but it dominates hers.
Gift and curse, all wrapped
in the same paper and ribbon.
Who gets to unwrap it?
Hangers-on, the insincere,
lust-driven troglodytes,
those who try way too hard.
She must weed through
this unkempt garden daily,
Eve to countless serpents,
hissing sad serenades
in tired trite routines,
unlike how she
and varsity teammates
execute flyer into cradle catch,
tucking and tumbling
in surprising athletic turns
for crowd's approval.

Male Order

Peruse our catalogue of curious mementos,
shells of shadows, quaint dreams turned to dust,

the soft wisp of a turtle's breath, a pine cone,
a messenger's abandoned pager, a deer's tooth,

the quiet perfume of an autumn day,
the scent of leaves and ripe apples falling,

your favorite sweater from 1980,
the one with the inexplicable white stripe,

a chamberlain's missive to a crier,
a sand bank full of youthful spirit,

the confidence of a first seat belt,
the cold heavy pleasure of a bucket

weighed down with soapy escapades,
a money-back guarantee for a small mirror,

one to show the truths of yesteryear,
tears of misunderstanding, the allure

of the neighbor's freckled smile,
those promises called out without echo

lost in canyons behind the reservoir,
like an approximation at humor. Order now

and get the bonus of a trampled heart,
before the personal wall was built,

back when love was a feasible concept,
when a million songs still were sung.

Collapse of the Center

She's silken, but not resembling a tent,
except when gathering disparate notions
to ponder, posture, adopt, circumvent,
like waves upon the storm-crossed oceans.
Nothing here can ever truly be owned,
these countless lies, those capricious whims,
these media models, perfectly coiffed and toned,
infinite hours spent in unmentioned gyms.
Loose approximations pass as tether,
binding us equally in fears and glory,
this digital realm pretends to draw together,
but communication is complex story.
The quirks of fate, the glitch gone viral,
the online world in downward spiral.

Geometry

She hits ground running,
racing against personal best,
challenging setting sun with
brows knit in furrowed concern.
Orange circle drops to horizon
as if weighted with gravitas
of adult responsibility.
Points of light on shadowed wall
mark obscure constellation
of recent love triangle.
The heavens mock
her wrecked tangle;
mind connects the dots,
measuring, recounting
vision of a vertex.
She is eager to find
reliable solution,
an equivalence relationship,
a formula to calculate
an area of safety,
means of escaping
this passion's trapezoid
and getting back
to square one.

Four

SALVATIONS

Contingent Occurrence

It is a mystery of flux and electrons.
Each moment a new beginning,
one that language might undermine
as we follow, seeking only to recognize.

We fail to communicate, awkward silence
filling precarious maze of shared ignorance.
These are secrets of dreams and lives lived.
There is language, process, orders to follow.

This is the hot precision of sunlight
illuminating a dark room's corner,
streaming like sin into hidden crannies,
then dissipating, ambition into sleep.

Close touch is shared nuance,
slow parade next to tranquil ocean,
a means of becoming unbecoming,
a love letter unopened on the bureau,
a kiss that looms and hovers, unrealized,
a lifetime writing pleasures unknown.

Exit Strategy

From edge we see
canyon's depths:
it is a long trek down,
and already we're racing sunset.
Better to depart back
through forest trail,
follow long shadows
beneath evergreen canopy,
searching for peace
and a way to forget
between prowling
of angry hawks.
They fly toward oblivion,
refusing to be tamed,
true to feral instincts
while we meander,
pondering a catalogue of sins
destined to define us,
irresponsible explorers
in this lifetime of regret.

The Uncoupling

From remnants of the unresolved,
comes sage insistence:
each beginning contains an end.
There is over time a slow degeneration,
fire to ash to earth wherein
wind wears down protective panes,
and drafts stir the hardest foundations.
Such a wind blows hard
this late afternoon,
shaking maple branches
to warn a sleeping garden
of nature's fickle dance.
Seasons come undone
as rhythms are thrown,
and even rising constellations
cast cautionary nods
toward reckless aftermath
on this planet of change.

Metaphor

Early October, a meaningless game
at the end of a horrible season,
an expensive first row ticket
behind the photographer's press box.
From this vantage point
the well-tended diamond looks approachable,
invitingly close, human.
Between inning practice throws
sizzle in from third to first.
Each audible pop in the fielder's mitt
saves me from unspeakable dangers,
foul balls or errant line drives.
The barrage and sonic rumble of low-flying planes
adds to the sensory overload, the carnival atmosphere.
All seems crisp, clean, otherworldly clear.

A pointless fall victory
from ragtag boys of summer,
a solid outing from a pitcher
returned from the disabled list,
a pair of two-run homers sparking enthusiasm
for a season yet to come.

When my team was heading off the field,
the second baseman sought a likely target
for a souvenir ball. When our eyes met, did he recognize
the look of a long suffering, die-hard fanatic,
did he hear the whispers of my frustration
at his season-long batting woes?
Did he feel the shared pain from when
he inexplicably dropped the routine pop-up
against the hated crosstown rivals?

He saw me, recognized something, and threw.
My right hand caught it barehanded,
and suddenly the eager college kid to my right had it too,
forcing it out of my one-handed grasp,
into his own waiting hands.
I didn't make a scene. I acquiesced
with the grace of knowing such a memento
was of no real use to me.

That ball was much like this season: promising,
firmly in hand, and soon wrested away.
We both lost out to others who wanted it more,
who did whatever it took
to come away with the prize.
Still, baseball is a forgiving game,
each long season soon followed by off-season moves,
then a spring of renewed hope and promise.
We loyal fans root on, enticed by possibility,
always willing to nobly suffer the slings and arrows
of the next outrageous season's fortune.

Siren

His red badge was not for courage,
but for dreaming and surviving
doomed battles of odd rebellion,
troops chanting rallying cries while
marching into distant remote silence.

Extant whispers arrived on winds
gleaned from inferred meanings
of pressed flowers and crinoline daydreams,
long nights of soundless longing,
celebrating bushels full of cravings.

But there is no life left to explore,
no fire crackling heat to melt regrets,
no mending flames to do a body good.
He abandoned them for a collection
of wild expressions, the lure of her

knowing smile, Southern charm
drawing him in like pealing bells from
charmed carillon, serenading love's ideal
as possible, all-encompassing magic.
Embracing possibilities of tactile extension,

satin silkiness of garments discarded,
dropped like hints leading to unraveled
satisfactions, sapping strength while
channeling blood away from brain
to another realm of assumed control.

Winter slumbers travel slowly and this
frigid January makes those summer
escapades seem like bitter fictions.
He stares at a daguerreotype, trying
to guess at what shadows are hiding.

History is elusive illusion, subjectively
manipulated by those controlling
narrative, not revealing
personal thirst, the how and why
of scattered wants and promises.

Her confession is a request
for absolution from the specific.
She wants him to forget her name,
but lose himself to shared pleasure.
Both undone like buttons.

In nightmares, his war becomes hers.
She hears names of victims,
of innocence tortured and turned
all manner of ugly, maimed
with scars of failed inquisition.

She knows such men won't escape
horrid throes of conscience,
in fitful nights of long eternity,
a religion of remorse and betrayal,
a means of young become old.

—continued

It is evident through their hunger
to please and appease, to atone
for filling graveyards with markers,
through sobbing when no one listens.
She cannot help but hear them all.

So she gives herself to service of
sustained impressions of affection,
providing moments of martyred hope
in spirit of camaraderie and prayer,
touch as familiar as weekly hymn.
Enticing those who cannot temper

carnal urges, such basic needs,
removing them from their worst selves
with tendered mercy of a savior
and providing succor to the living
on behalf of those conscripted to die.

Filling moon tempts feral dogs
to howling reverence, packs of
canines awaiting signals only they
can discern, songs of instinct
from the alpha barking orders.

Her tune is different, a ballad
of soft amnesty and sweet forgiveness,
sense memory and redolent whimsy.
While he owes her his life and livelihood,
it's something he'll never discover.

Soft Magic

The large man
on the elevator
makes sure all
the women enter
and exit before him.
He wishes everyone
a blessed day ahead.
The young woman
standing so close
on the overly crowded
downtown express train
is oblivious
to my reading
what she texts
on her phone.
It is in Chinese—
privacy is protected.
The lanky Dominican
wags a finger,
looking out
for his elderly Papi
sitting across the way.
He serves up a smile
as our eyes meet.
At my stop,
I wish him
a great day.
This is the circle
of kindness
not publicized,

—continued

the soft magic
of the city,
its melting pot
of various peoples,
all going about
their respective business,
but paying forward
good wishes that make
the daily challenges
of the harsh metropolis
that much easier to bear.
You too, my friend,
he answers back.
The doors close behind me,
but the day is just beginning.

Deliver Us from What We've Become

Truth becomes a churlish notion
in hands of unholy crew,
setting course for deeper ocean
beyond straits of misconstrue.
Never stop to ask directions,
always earn a tidy sum.
Bless the workers' genuflections
under watchful leader's thumb.
Pay to grab inside advantage
as prelude to righteous rage,
don't get caught applying bandage
(wounds are tendered to off-stage).
Here the story's never ending,
there the money lands offshore,
follow where the bank is lending,
under every stone explore.
Bully for this extradition,
kudos to the watchful eye.
Lying is the new tradition:
never give the reason why.
Act as if it's all expected,
so much for this sleight of hand,
what they hope went undetected
turns up with a new demand.
Headlines turn outrageous folly
into depths of soulless ice,
Deaf ears never seemed so jolly
when evading sound advice.
Fiction seen as real creation,
pulling wool over the eyes,

—continued

accolade as accusation,
rich reward of peaceful prize.
When shall sound the judge's gavel?
When shall justice rear its head?
Every day new threads unravel,
greater runs the flow of dread.
Watch, we watch and wait and wonder,
bracing for the iceberg's cross,
hoping that this spell we're under
breaks before the mounting loss.
We the people want solutions
reckoning approaching soon,
fast before our institutions
fall apart in wrack and ruin.

Caesura

Now he understands
why they say be careful
what you wish for.

His whole high school career
he wished for this,
a class full of the prettiest,

a veritable parade
of pristine pulchritude
to divert and distract,

feed the nightly fantasies,
provide the lore of
endless adolescent yearning.

Yet now nature's nasty secret
is teased out as slow reveal.
This lovely tableau unravels

when mouths open to unleash
torrents of trivial self-importance
of bloated egos and idiocy mingling

in revealing detail
about upcoming prom choices
through overtly exaggerated drama:

boyfriends and spray-on tans,
inanity posing as conversation,
the madness of the commonplace,

—continued

not a thought approaching
Heidegger's ontological questions
regarding being in the world.

Instead this truth unmasked
makes him wish anew for silent films,
a diminishment of volume.

Beauty's ugly side is exposed
in giggling comments
of superior attitudes and judgments.

This unlikely realization
draws him unexpectedly
away from the noisy commotion

to that quiet plain one,
off by herself
in the opposite corner,

perhaps contemplating
Hegel's absolute idealism,
immanence, transcendence.

Her silent smile
invites him to stop
and rethink the world

of pointless wishes
he had been raised to relish.
Wiser now from knowledge

that beauty emanates
from within to without,
he knows the reverse
doesn't always follow.

Cathedral

Sometimes one is fooled by stillness
into thinking this place is infused by spirits
and a higher power's transcendence.
Solitude as charade, enhanced by the smell of
waving censers, clouds of holy aroma
dispersed as someone enters from the rear.
A chalice fills with blood as votive smoke,
one large word balloon, rises toward rafters.
I hide among regulars, a sinner pretending,
lost in thought, trying to undo life's tangles.
I imagine a short run to liberty.
Beside quickened heartbeat's echoes,
no earthly trace of what went before,
no hungry mouths to feed or provide for,
merely an illusion of heavenly do-over,
a sweet oasis from this burning desert,
away from constricting yokes
that tie me to a daily burden
of blessedly deadened existence.

Volume Two

It's a long way across black waters
to where you softly whisper your rumors,
spin moonlight into gossamer and innuendo,
excite readers into shared adventures
that we'd all like to believe happened.
How many would be disappointed
to look into those eyes and find them cold,
emptied of the wild heat that once made
a four-poster bed into a kingdom's throne.
Now there is a tired bemusement,
a calculated tolerance that produces,
sitting at this oversized wooden surface
as sole member of this linguistic assembly line,
placing adjectives and prepositions,
an absent-minded Eiffel, turning phrases
into variants of what came before,
hoping no one discovers what they lack.

Macchu Pichu of Your Mind

The erotic tapestry lay unfurled
in the corner, stuck in time,
a frozen image seeking eyes, reactions,
as when pillagers invaded Holy Land
and found it inexplicably deserted,
or when Euripides broached topics
so very taboo that actors refused
to speak the words, that sordid tale
of man, maid, gods and sea serpents,
a crowded chariot to the underworld,
chaotic and cursed, now lost to history,
which is to say relax a bit,
appreciate stillness, silence,
temptation of woven tableau,
and let me know if you care to visit Peru
anytime soon.

Resignation

She says she's fine with compromise.
She is cavalier, noncommittal.
I am familiar with destruction
left in her careless wake.
She carries more attitude
than she ever needs.

This patriotic sun
bathes me in its angry fervor.
She has taught me
the important lesson of failure,
dissolution of a national dream.
The force majeure of obliterated
plans, reset button pressed
following lightning strike.
I am out of options.

Stability is the grand illusion.
Seismic readiness only goes so far.
When crisis arrives,
hearts pack passports
and go. And go. And go.
Coded messages remain unsolved
as today meets forever,
beating to mock the beaten,
white flags waving in wind.

Alchemy

This tenuous flirtation,
the costs of acting coy,
whispering as if volume
could shout denial,
yet nothing cancels out.
This poverty of reason
subverted by emotion
converts thought to fantasy,
to smattering cacophony of nasty scenario.
He, convinced he has
willed her into existence,
conjured from prior thought
into flesh and hot blood,
believes the impossible,
through mundane messages
read over and over to
yield hidden meanings.
This pitiful desperate
grandeur of delusion
is exercise in modern futility,
sugar-coated by platitudes
and a string of complex emojis.
This ego massage lasts only so long,
then rubs the wrong way,
dead bouquet in graveyard,
strewn by strong winds
and sotto voce goodbye.

Zeros

Cold beyond feeling,
a dampening of sensate ways
toward surprisingly soothing
glacial numb comfort
that adds up on this icy plane
where crampons tread carefully,
creakily advancing where
heartbeats ride addled blows
of slow arctic perambulation,
hard breath writing cloud messages,
your gloved hand in mine
tethered for safety together,
insulated beyond simple touch,
climbing to heights unknown.

Dunwoodie

So I had to return
to the scene of the crime.
That crime was my teenage years.
That scene was the local pizzeria,
the popular hangout back in the day.
It hadn't changed much
in the decades since
my last visit:
same cramped quarters,
same small tables,
still quality slices.
Voted best pizza
in the county
by a small landslide.
Some things never change.
I inquired after Gabe,
the ever-cheery and
convivial co-owner
who used to ask,
"What size soda,
big or large?"
He had a stroke about six years ago,
and can no longer speak.
But his mind is still fine.
Some things change a little.
I order a slice of Sicilian,
double baked and stuffed
full of melted mozzarella.
A corner slice, of course.
Those in the know want
the crunch and the crackle.

Every bite is a gift of
melted cheese and memories.
I see the regulars of now,
not much changed from
the ones of bygone then.
I look out the plate glass,
knowing there's always a hunger:
to return, to change the past,
to try and make things right.

Reminder #17

Lonely promontory on craggy coast
where some anonymous artist
has created unlikely balanced piles
of flat gray rocks to populate this
godforsaken end of the earth
with Giacometti-like shadows,
thin specters that haunt and serve
to remind that even in this
most remote of nautical byways,
there is art and the beneficial illusion
that we are not alone.

Indirections

This collateral excursion
takes us far from our destination,
hugging mountainside
like some discrete entities
having lost a sense of how to climb.
This road map is a colorful cipher,
a fastidious tablature revealing little.
Topographically, we remain inclined
to slope, differentiating in approximate
languages that make further iterations necessary.
Driver, please stop. Turn around.
Change what keeps us awake nights.
Decelerate our alleged independence:
it's all downhill from here.

Postscript

The famous poet was sitting on his hotel bed naked.
My head told me to blame the San Francisco he had known.

This was a different world, not necessarily a better one.
I lit another votive candle to define my personal space.

He stroked his stubble and seemed to be deep in thought.
I had been warned about his gruff proclamations of regrets.

At this late stage, he was mostly vituperative bluster,
but somewhere in there were remnants of a once great mind.

He was confused: was I a reporter, a suitor, a fan, a potential lover?
I let the silence respond and tried not to judge.

Heroes grow old, but rarely stop publishing.
Long after their muse has fled, blather fills pages.

I nodded my head and listened more for the man he once was
than the grousing spectacle cursing the universe around him.

I conjured respect from deep within my aging poetic heart,
knowing someday that old naked man might be me.

About the Author

Gary Glauber is a poet, fiction writer, teacher, and former music journalist and sportswriter. His poetry and fiction have garnered multiple nominations for the Pushcart Prize and Best of the Net. An expansive variety of literary journals, magazines, and anthologies feature Glauber's published poems and stories. This is his fourth full length poetry collection, joining *Small Consolations* (Aldrich Press), *Worth the Candle* (Five Oaks Press), and *Rocky Landscape with Vagrants* (Cyberwit); and two chapbooks, *Memory Marries Desire* (Finishing Line Press) and *The Covalence of Equanimity* (SurVision Books), a winner of the 2019 James Tate International Poetry Prize. He continues to champion the underdog while negotiating life's absurdities.

Shanti Arts

Nature ▪ Art ▪ Spirit

Please visit us online
to browse our entire book catalog,
including poetry collections and fiction,
books on travel, nature, healing, art,
photography, and more.

Also take a look at our highly
regarded art and literary journal,
Still Point Arts Quarterly, which
may be downloaded for free.

www.shantiarts.com

www.ingramcontent.com/pod-product-compliance
Lightning Source LLC
Chambersburg PA
CBHW070449050426
42451CB00015B/3407